Amazing Crime Scene Science

SEARCHING FOR MURDER CLUES

John Townsend

amicus

Published by Amicus
P.O. Box 1329
Mankato, MN 56002

Printed in the United States of America at Corporate Graphics, in North Mankato, Minnesota.

Library of Congress Cataloging-in-Publication Data
Townsend, John, 1955-
  Searching for murder clues / by John Townsend.
    p. cm. -- (Amazing crime scene science)
  Includes bibliographical references and index.
  Summary: "Explains how crime scene investigation experts use evidence and science to identify murder victims,
  determine when and how they were killed, and track down who committed the murder. Includes case files and case
  studies of real murder cases"--Provided by publisher.
  ISBN 978-1-60753-172-2 (library binding)
  1. Murder--Investigation--Juvenile literature. 2. Homicide investigation--Juvenile literature. I. Title.
  HV8079.H6T69 2012
  363.25'9523--dc22
                                2010033804

Appleseed Editions, Ltd.
Created by Q2AMedia
Editor: Katie Dicker
Art Director: Harleen Mehta
Designer: Cheena Yadav, Neha Kaul
Picture Researchers: Debabrata Sen, Rajeev Parmar

All words in **bold** can be found in the Glossary on pages 30–31.

Picture credits
t=top b=bottom c=center— l=left r=right

Jubal Harshaw/Shutterstock, Timothy R. Nichols/Shutterstock: Title page, Dmitry Nikolajchuk/Shutterstock: Contents page,
Karen Moskowitz/Stone/Getty Images: 4, Corepics/Istockphoto: 5, Adam Gault/Photolibrary: 6, David Quinn/AP Photo: 7,
 Mauro Fermariello/Science Photo Library: 8, Bonita Cheshier/Dreamstime: 9c, Sebastian Kaulitzki/Shutterstock: 9b,
Luminis/Shutterstock: 10, Rex Features: 11, Frontier Henri/Istockphoto: 12, Miroslav Jelinek www.regardit.eu: 13,
Drzaribu/Dreamstime: 14, Henrik Jonsson/Istockphoto: 15bl, James Steidl/Shutterstock: 15br, Dmitriy Cherevko/
Dreamstime: 16, Michealofiachra/Istockphoto: 17, Courtesy of Daniel Muzio: 18, Henri et George/Shutterstock: 19t, Regis
Martin/Getty Images: 19c, Sipa Press/Rex Features: 19b, Benne Ochs/Photolibrary: 20, Institute of Forensic Medicine,
University of Bern: 21, HO Old/Reuters: 22, Dudarev Mikhail/Shutterstock: 23t, Undergroundarts.co.uk/Shutterstock: 23c,
Louisa Howard, Charles Daghlian: 24, South Tyrol Museum of Archaeology - www.iceman.it: 25, Volker Steger/
Photolibrary: 26, Hintau Aliaksei/Shutterstock: 27t, HO Old/Reuters: 27c, Jubal Harshaw/Shutterstock, Timothy R.
Nichols/Shutterstock: 27b, Alexis Rosenfeld/Science Photo Library: 28, Steve Gschmeissner/Science Photo Library: 29,
Henrik Jonsson/Istockphoto: 31.
Cover images: Gary Conner/Photolibrary, Theo Hawkins/Istockphoto, Leah-Anne Thompson/Shutterstock, Andrea Danti/
Shutterstock.

DAD0052
3-2011

9 8 7 6 5 4 3 2 1

CONTENTS

The Silent Witness

In crime stories, television shows, and real life, some murderers think they can commit the perfect murder. They believe they can hide all the clues linking them to a crime. They're usually wrong!

A Perfect Murder?

If no one sees the murder, if the crime scene shows no signs of violence, and if the body is carefully hidden, the murderer is unlikely to get caught—or so you might think. **Forensic** experts can still get to the truth. The remains of a body tend to be discovered eventually. Although a dead body cannot say what happened, it can still tell the police a great deal from its many clues.

Even if a dead body is hidden in a remote place, it is likely to be found eventually —and forensic experts soon get to work.

When a Dead Body Speaks

Forensic scientists often can discover who the **victim** was and figure out if the cause of death was natural, accidental, suicide, or murder.

In a murder case, the **CSI** (crime scene investigation) team investigates who the killer might be. If the victim was killed recently, an **autopsy** can reveal many hidden clues.

This book explains how forensic experts search for murder clues and uncover all kinds of hidden **evidence**.

A body and scattered evidence at a crime scene soon give the CSI team plenty of clues to the murder.

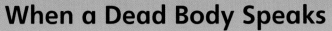
DID YOU KNOW?

A **pathologist** can discover many clues about a murder by examining the victim's remains. Important evidence can be gathered from a **corpse** and its organs, tissue, bones, teeth, blood, injuries, insects, **bacteria,** and all manner of stomach secrets!

Who Is It?

The first questions the CSI experts have to answer are: Who are the victims? When did they die? How did they die?

At the Scene

Before anyone can move a dead body or skeleton, its position is recorded with notes, sketches, measurements, and photographs. Close-up pictures will show details of any wounds or the position of weapons. The body will be examined for **trace evidence** and then taken away in a body bag for an autopsy.

A skull can give important clues to the identity of a victim and how the murder was carried out.

SCIENCE SECRETS

Clues from a skull:
- The chin is squarer in the skull of a man and slightly more pointed in a woman.
- The forehead of a male's skull slants backward, while a female's head is usually more rounded.
- Males have **brow ridges** but females do not.

Important Clues

As well as examining the body's wounds, limbs, and organs, the pathologist collects any material under the fingernails and in the ears or nose. Fingerprints are also taken. Sometimes, **X-rays** show previous injuries or bone fractures that can be checked against local hospital records to identify the victim.

The victim's clothes give further clues, such as the contents of pockets and name tags. Invisible ink, sometimes used to mark a person's clothes or other possessions, will show under an **ultraviolet** light.

A skeleton can reveal a victim's size, sex, race, and sometimes country of origin. New forensic science can examine the minerals in bones and match them to various drinking waters found around the world.

Forensic officers use a body bag to remove a dead body from the scene of a crime.

After these detailed examinations, a pathologist can often learn who the victim was, the time and cause of death, and even uncover clues that may identify the murderer.

Body Clues

Some murderers will try anything to get rid of a dead body—even cutting it up. By scattering the body parts, they hope the police will be unable to identify the victim's body. But they would be surprised.

Skin Secrets

Many unknown corpses have been identified by their fingertips, where the skin has a **unique** pattern of tiny ridges. If the dead person was a criminal, it's likely that the fingerprints were already on police records.

Sometimes, a dead person can be identified by other unique marks. Birthmarks and old scars can be so unusual that a relative of a missing person can identify them with certainty. Tattoos are particularly useful in this way because some designs include special dates or symbols.

An autopsy is carried out on a body to try to determine the cause of death.

CASE FILE

In 1935, at a sea life park in New South Wales, Australia, the crowd watched a shark through the glass of its tank and gasped in horror. The shark, which had recently been caught out at sea, suddenly coughed out a human arm.

When the police recovered the arm and examined it, they saw it had not been bitten off at the shoulder but cut off cleanly with a knife. The victim must have been murdered, cut up, and thrown into the ocean. But who was the victim?

The police took fingerprints and discovered that the arm belonged to a **criminal** named James Smith, whose wife had reported him missing. She was asked to identify the arm because it had an unusual tattoo. She was certain the arm belonged to her missing husband.

A murder inquiry began and **suspects** were arrested, but nothing could be proved and the famous shark arm case remains unsolved.

Do you have a distinguishing mark that could identify your body?

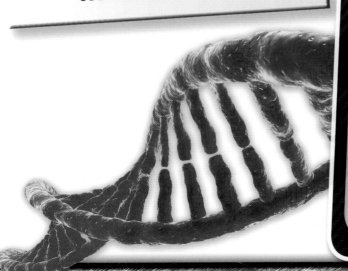

SCIENCE SECRETS

Since the mid-1980s, scientists have been able to identify some murder victims from just a few body **cells**. A substance in all cells, called **DNA**, can be tested and matched against police records. This **genetic** fingerprinting is possible because everyone's DNA is different, except for some identical twins.

The Woman in the Suitcase

The task of identifying a badly **decomposed** body is difficult enough—but tracking down the murderer takes amazing skill and clever science.

Grisly Discovery

In 2001, a person walking near York, United Kingdom, noticed an old suitcase. The person was horrified to discover that the case contained the rotting remains of a human body.

A pathologist examined the remains and figured out that the victim was a female in her twenties who had been **suffocated**. Tests on her hair showed that she was from southeast Asia. But there was nothing to indicate who she was because her fingerprints and dental records matched no information held in the United Kingdom.

What would you do if you discovered a suspicious suitcase?

Mystery Solved

The Korean Embassy in London sent the British police the fingerprints of a Korean student who was missing in Britain. She was 21-year-old Hyo Jung Jin and her fingerprints matched those of the body in the suitcase. Her missing bank card had been used to take money from her bank account.

The police soon linked Hyo Jung Jin to another female Korean student. The suffocated body of In Hea Song had been found in a closet in a house in London belonging to a man named Kyo Soo Kim. As he had known both victims, Kyo Soo Kim became a suspect. Forensic scientists began to find strong evidence linking him to both murders:

- Blue paint from Kyo Soo Kim's house matched blue paint on the suitcase hiding Hyo Jung Jin's body.
- Traces of Hyo Jung Jin's blood were found on Kyo Soo Kim's floor, walls, bed, and car.
- Hyo Jung Jin's DNA was on items in the closet hiding In Hea Song's body.

In 2003, Kyo Soo Kim was found guilty of both murders and sent to prison for life.

In Hea Song, age 22, was reported missing in December 2001. Her body was discovered the following March.

CAN YOU BELIEVE IT?

The murderer had tied Hyo Jung Jin's body in a rare type of sticky tape. A roll of this tape was found at Kyo Soo Kim's house. The tape around Hyo Jung Jin's wrists showed traces of orange paint, which exactly matched paint found on Kyo Soo Kim's T-shirt.

Time of Death

Knowing exactly when a murder victim was killed is vital information in any murder investigation. Sometimes, a lot of forensic work is needed to learn the exact time of death.

Scientists are able to determine the age of skeletal remains found buried in the soil.

Fixing the Time

By taking the temperature of a recently murdered body, a pathologist will be able to work out how long the victim has been dead. In normal conditions, a body will cool by 2.7°F (1.5°C) per hour.

Rigor mortis is another way to figure out the time of death. When a person dies, the muscles stiffen. The process normally begins 2 hours after death and can last up to 48 hours.

SCIENCE SECRETS

A technique called **radiocarbon dating** can give the age of skeletal remains. But forensic scientists have also developed a new carbon dating method for finding the age of corpses. It measures the amount of radioactive carbon in the lens of a person's eye to measure how long ago they were born. This can be done up to three days after death.

Insect Clues

The rate at which insects feed on a dead body can give useful clues to a pathologist. Within an hour of the victim's death, blowflies are likely to lay their eggs on parts of the body. The eggs will hatch within 24 hours. The maggots will grow to just over 0.4 inch (1 cm) as they feed on the body for about 12 days before turning into adult flies. An insect expert takes all this into account, knowing that flies do not lay eggs at night and are slower to lay eggs in cooler temperatures.

The grisly work of collecting flies and maggots from a corpse is an important part of forensic murder investigations. It may seem like an unpleasant job, but measuring the rate of decay of a dead body provides vital clues. This important work has helped to catch many murderers—as the next case study shows.

Blowflies lay their eggs on the remains of a dead animal or human within an hour of death.

Maggots Trap a Killer

In 1993, a murderer in Mississippi thought he had committed the perfect crime by proving he was far away from the murder scene at the time. But maggots proved he lied.

A Killer Strikes

In mid-December, Michael Rubenstein called the police to tell them he'd found the bodies of three of his relatives in a remote cabin near the small town of Summit. The police arrived to find the murdered bodies had clearly been dead for many days. Michael Rubenstein told the police that he'd last visited the cabin two weeks earlier and another two weeks before that. Both times, he'd had no concerns about his relatives. They were his stepson Darryl (age 24), Darryl's wife Evelyn (age 20), and their daughter Krystal (age 4).

Wriggling maggots usually mean rotting remains are close by.

Suspicious Dealings

The police began to wonder about Rubenstein's story when he tried to collect his stepson's **life insurance** money. But Rubenstein had witnesses to prove he had been nowhere near the murder scene for two weeks. The police then wondered if the bodies could have been lying there for *more* than two weeks. Forensic scientists were called in to figure out the exact time of the deaths.

CSI experts examined the murder scene and found maggots in the bodies. They also discovered the time of death was *four* weeks before—exactly when Rubenstein had admitted visiting the cabin.

In **court**, an insect expert explained how the size of the maggots in the bodies proved the victims had been dead for more than two weeks. They were killed much earlier than Rubenstein's last visit to the cabin when he claimed that nothing was amiss. Rubenstein was found guilty of the murders and sentenced to death.

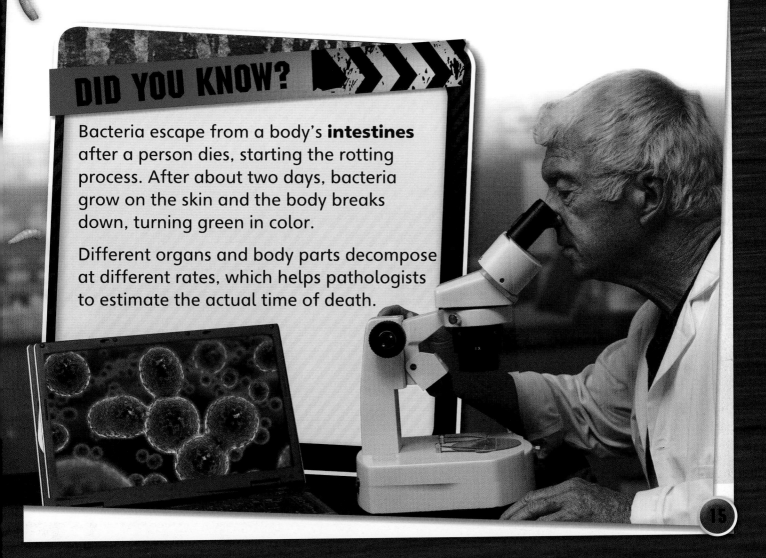

DID YOU KNOW?

Bacteria escape from a body's **intestines** after a person dies, starting the rotting process. After about two days, bacteria grow on the skin and the body breaks down, turning green in color.

Different organs and body parts decompose at different rates, which helps pathologists to estimate the actual time of death.

Killer Tactics

Finding out who a dead person was, as well as the time of death, can be difficult for the CSI team. Is it easier to find out how the victim was killed? Not always!

Investigating Injuries

If a murder victim was hit, shot, or stabbed, obvious signs are likely. Any violent blow to a person is called blunt force trauma, which usually leaves severe wounds. But death may be due to internal injuries with few signs other than bruises.

Sometimes, a body shows no evidence of an attack at all, and it may not be clear what actually caused the death. If so, it is the pathologist's job to examine the body very carefully. Some murderers try to disguise the cause of death by making it look like an accident.

No Sign of Injury

If there are no clear clues to the cause of death, experts look for signs of **asphyxiation**, such as bloodshot eyes or strangle marks around the neck. An autopsy shows if the brain was starved of oxygen and whether body tissues show a deadly buildup of **carbon dioxide**.

The color of a victim's blood can also show whether the victim was gassed. Poisoning used to be a common method of murder, but modern science can test a victim's blood and stomach contents to learn exactly what the poison was and how much was used.

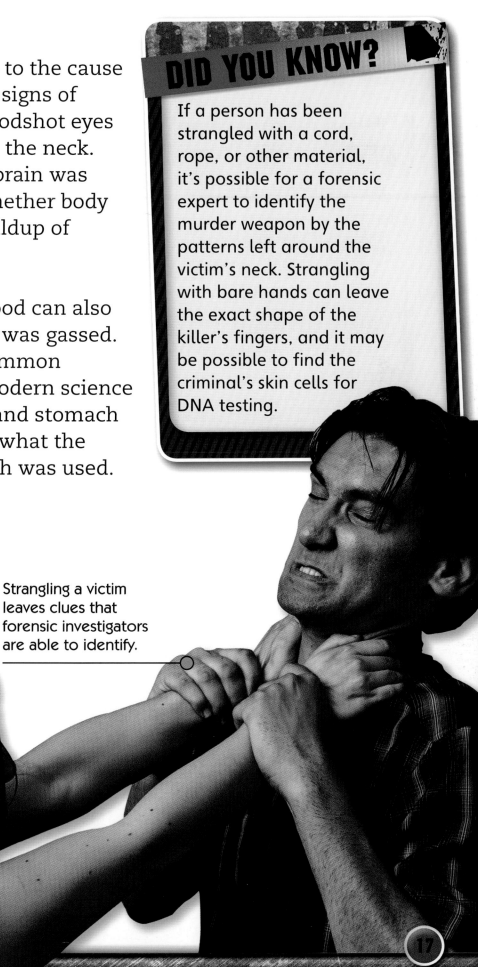

DID YOU KNOW?

If a person has been strangled with a cord, rope, or other material, it's possible for a forensic expert to identify the murder weapon by the patterns left around the victim's neck. Strangling with bare hands can leave the exact shape of the killer's fingers, and it may be possible to find the criminal's skin cells for DNA testing.

Strangling a victim leaves clues that forensic investigators are able to identify.

17

Broken Bones

When all that remains of a murder victim are the bones, it would seem impossible to find out what killed them. Amazingly, thanks to CSI teams, it can be done.

Bone Detectives

A fractured skull suggests the victim was hit on the head and suffered blunt force trauma. Any holes in the skull might show if the victim was shot in the head. The size of these holes gives bone experts an idea of the type of bullets used and even the make of gun. If any of the ribs or the breastbone show cut marks, it is likely the victim was stabbed in the chest. These clues, as well as any broken bones, can begin to reveal how a person was attacked.

Scientists study the bones in mass graves to determine what happened to the victims.

CAN YOU BELIEVE IT?

Finding clues in bones can be like solving a giant puzzle, especially when many skeletons are buried together. A forensic **anthropologist** must sort out the bone parts, separate them from soil and stones, take them back to a laboratory, clean them up, fit them all together, and then study them.

CASE FILE

Clea Koff calls herself "the bone woman" because she's a forensic anthropologist. As Koff says, "We are able to interpret marks and changes on the bones to find what diseases or trauma they suffered during life and at the moment of death. Teeth are a particular interest of mine—they tell us a lot."

In 1996, Koff was chosen by the **United Nations** to go to Rwanda in Africa to unearth evidence of war crimes committed two years earlier. She pieced together the human remains from mass graves and figured out what happened to the victims. She discovered that the skeletons were women and children. Many of the ankle bones had been hacked by **machetes**. This gave important evidence to help find the killers.

Clea Koff studies human skeletons and bones.

Forensic scientists examine the bones of unidentified people to help figure out who they are and how they died.

Who Did It?

Where would you begin searching for clues to reveal the identity of a murderer? Believe it or not, there may be very clear signs on the victim's body.

Biting Clues

Sometimes, it is possible for forensic experts to look at stab wounds and determine if a murderer was right or left handed and even the murderer's height and strength. There may be more clues. In some attacks, the murderer and victim struggle and fight. If they end up biting each other, each is left with telltale teeth marks.

A bite mark can be linked to the victim or the murderer.

CAN YOU BELIEVE IT?

Carmine Calabro, a murderer in New York, bit his victim. When he was arrested in 1979, dental experts matched his teeth to the bite-mark bruises on the victim's body. Since this would be key evidence at the trial, Calabro tried to destroy the proof by pulling out all his teeth! It didn't help though—he still got a life sentence.

One of the most famous U.S. murder cases where a bite mark led to a **conviction** occured in 1979. This was before DNA evidence could be used.

A mass murderer, Ted Bundy, attacked many women in the 1970s by hitting them over the head and strangling them to death. In 1978, Bundy killed two women at Florida State University and left two others seriously injured.

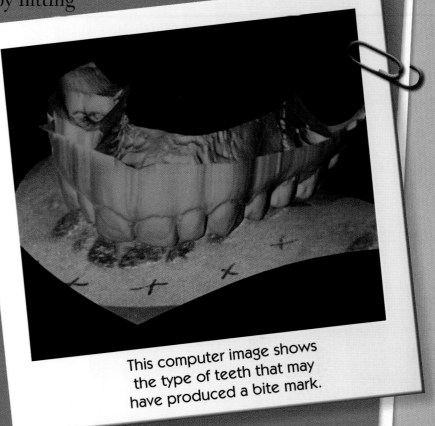

This computer image shows the type of teeth that may have produced a bite mark.

When a witness described the attacker, the police tracked down the man, who was an escaped prisoner. Ted Bundy was put on trial. A vital piece of evidence against him was a bite mark found on the body of one of the victims.

In court, an enlarged photograph of the bite mark was shown next to an image of Bundy's front teeth. His chipped and uneven teeth had a distinct outline. A forensic dentist explained how the photograph of the bite mark matched Bundy's teeth exactly. This proved Bundy was the attacker, and he was found guilty. He was **executed** in 1989 after confessing to more than 30 murders.

Beyond All Doubt

In some modern murder investigations, all the clues can create such strong evidence that the killer, or killers, have no chance of getting away with murder.

Vicious Attack

Just after Christmas in 2002, 31-year-old Kevin Jackson ran out of his house in Yorkshire, United Kingdom, to chase three men who were trying to steal his father-in-law's jeep. The men stabbed him in the head and ran off. Kevin died from his wounds two days later.

From their investigation and witness statements, the police soon wanted to question a suspect, but it seemed unlikely that they would find any evidence from such a short, sudden attack. However, there were plenty of clues.

Kevin Jackson died trying to protect his family's property. He had a wife and two young sons.

The Evidence Mounts

The CSI team discovered:

- A forensic scientist examined the suspect's car and found a screwdriver with microscopic traces of blood on it. DNA tests matched the blood to the murder victim.

- The same screwdriver matched the marks inside the lock of the jeep that the gang had been trying to steal.

- Three weeks after the murder, the police arrested two more suspects and found further evidence in their homes. This included a pair of boots covered in blood spatters that matched the victim's DNA.

- These boots, as well as a pair of sneakers in the other suspect's house, matched footprints left in the snow at the murder scene.

- The suspects denied the footwear was theirs, but forensic tests found their skin cells and hairs inside.

The three suspects (Rashad Zaman, Rangzaib Akhtar, and Raees Khan) were all in their early twenties. From the evidence, they were convicted of murder and each received a life sentence in prison.

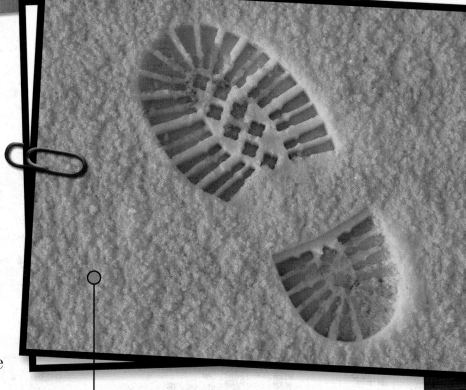

Footprints left in the snow were vital clues that helped to catch the killers.

SCIENCE SECRETS

A key piece of evidence in this case came from under the murder victim's fingernails. Kevin Jackson had scrapings from his attacker's skin, which DNA tests proved to belong to Raees Khan. The CSI team said this major evidence not only put the suspect at the crime scene but also proved that he had attacked the victim.

Telltale Pollen

Tiny particles from plants, often no bigger than grains of dust and visible only under a microscope, have helped forensic teams in their search for murder clues.

Invisible Clues

The **pollen** of every type of plant is different. When viewed under a microscope, pollen grains are like fingerprints because they identify a particular plant species. If forensic scientists find pollen on a body, they can tell where the victim had been by the plants he or she had brushed against. If the pollen is not from the surrounding area, the victim was probably moved from the murder scene. The pollen may even have come from the murderer's own yard!

Seen under a microscope, pollen grains can be linked to the scene of a murder.

DID YOU KNOW?

The study of pollen evidence in crime scene science is called forensic **palynology**. If you think this may be the job for you, you'll need to be good at science, know a lot about plants, and not have hay fever!

CASE FILE

In 1991, two mountain hikers in the snowy Alps of Austria came across a frozen body. Tests later revealed it had been dead for 5,300 years! Scientists discovered that the Iceman, as he became known, was in his forties when he died, which was old for those times.

How the Iceman died was a mystery at first. He had a chest wound and broken ribs, but the experts thought he must have died from the cold in midwinter. Inside his stomach, however, was pollen from a tree called a hop hornbeam. The Iceman had swallowed this just before he died— perhaps some pollen was on his food or had mixed with his saliva. This must have been in early summer, soon after hop hornbeam trees bloom.

An arrowhead found in the Iceman's shoulder proved he had been murdered by being hit in the back. He had pulled out the weapon, but the arrow's head remained stuck in his shoulder. He must have staggered to the top of the mountains and collapsed where he bled to death.

The Iceman was also known as Ötzi after the Ötztal area where he was found. His body was perfectly preserved in the ice.

Fibers that Catch Killers

Tiny strands from our clothes are left behind wherever we go. These cloth fibers, when studied under a microscope, can be perfect clues to a murder.

CSI Searches

One of the simplest pieces of equipment used by CSI teams is sticky tape. It is ideal for picking up almost invisible threads and fibers from a murder scene. Fibers from clothes, carpets, curtains, or any other fabric are easily transferred from one object to another.

Fibers found on a suspect can link him or her to a crime scene because fibers, like fingerprints, can have a unique pattern. To match fibers, scientists compare the fiber type, color, and the particular dye used.

Sticky tape is a useful tool to collect fiber samples from a crime scene.

CASE FILE

In July 2000, eight-year-old Sarah Payne went missing in Sussex, United Kingdom, while playing near her grandparents' home. Tragically, her murdered body was found not far away.

A local man with a police record was arrested as a suspect and linked to the murder from fiber evidence. More than 500 items were sent to crime laboratories for forensic testing. More than 20 forensic experts worked on the case. At the suspect's trial, key fiber evidence was presented in court:

- Fibers stuck to the **Velcro** on one of Sarah's shoes were from the suspect's red sweatshirt.

- Fibers from items in the suspect's van were found in Sarah's hair.

- DNA tests proved a hair found on the suspect's sweatshirt was Sarah's.

After 17 months of detailed forensic investigation, Roy Whiting was found guilty of this crime and sent to prison for life.

Sarah Payne was eight years old when she died.

DID YOU KNOW?

A sweater sheds fibers easily, but it also holds fibers from other clothes it touches. Most clothes will leave behind a few fiber fragments if they rub against a doorframe. Even a polished hit-and-run car will pick up tiny fragments of the victim's clothing.

What Next?

Amazing crime scene science continues to develop ways of searching for murder clues and tracking down murderers. What will forensic experts come up with next?

Future Forensics

One recent development in forensic science is the testing of hair samples. U.S. scientists can discover where a person lives in the United States based on traces of chemicals in a hair sample.

"Police are already using this method to find the origins of unidentified murder victims," a scientist from Utah said. He collected hair samples from barber shops in 65 U.S. cities and samples of the cities' tap water. The water you drink, which varies in different parts of the world, can be detected in your hair!

Who knows what secrets hide in your hair when magnified like this?

Underwater Research

If a murderer throws a body overboard from a boat, imagine how difficult it is for the CSI team to recover the victim and search for clues. The way a body decomposes under water is very different from on land. Studies help to show the rates of decay at different depths. A body thrown into the sea, for example, will rise from the seabed and float to the surface due to increasing gases inside the corpse.

Not all CSI work is as gruesome as this! Much of it is the routine and painstaking search for clues. But with the help of modern science, this important work will continue to put killers behind bars.

Recovering a body under the sea requires the CSI team to take great care to preserve, record, and collect the evidence, including using underwater photography.

CAN YOU BELIEVE IT?

To find out how bodies decay deep under water, scientists filmed a dead pig on the seabed. They monitored the water temperature, pressure, and sea creatures feeding on the body. Maggots feed on dead bodies on land, but scavengers of the sea are crabs and shrimps. Will you ever eat shrimp stir-fry again?

Glossary

anthropologist
someone who studies human beings and their physical characteristics

asphyxiation
death by lack of oxygen in the body, usually caused by lack of breathing

autopsy
an examination of a dead body especially to find out the cause of death

bacteria
microorganisms—some types of bacteria are active in the rotting process

brow ridges
bony ridges on the forehead

carbon dioxide
the waste gas we breathe out to keep our body healthy

cells
the basic building blocks of all living things, which are continually being renewed

conviction
when someone is proven guilty of a crime in court

corpse
a dead body

court
the place where a criminal is proven innocent or guilty

CSI
crime scene investigation

decompose
when something rots

DNA
the code in each person's cells that makes everyone unique

evidence
material presented to a court to prove the truth in a crime case

executed
when someone is put to death for a crime they have committed

forensic
scientific methods used to investigate and establish facts in criminal courts

genetic
controlled by genes, which are sets of instructions in all our body cells that make us who we are

intestines
the tubes of the digestive system where food is absorbed into the body

life insurance
money paid to
a named person
when the insured
person dies

machete
a large heavy knife
used for cutting
sugarcane or as
a weapon

palynology
the scientific study
of spores and pollen

pathologist
a forensic scientist
who examines
samples of
body tissue and
dead bodies

pollen
the powder found
inside flowers
that helps plants to
reproduce

radiocarbon dating
a way of measuring
the age of materials,
such as bones,
from the amount
of carbon 14 (a
chemical) found
in the material

rigor mortis
the temporary
stiffness of muscles
that occurs shortly
after death

suffocate
to die or suffer from
lack of oxygen

suspect
someone thought to
be guilty of a crime

trace evidence
small amounts of
material such as
hair, pollen grains,
or soil that can be
used as proof in a
crime investigation

ultraviolet
light that can
reveal blood and
fingerprints that
are not visible to
the naked eye

unique
only one like it in
the world

United Nations
an international
organization working
for world peace and
human rights

Velcro
a nylon fabric that
can be fastened to
itself—often used on
shoes and clothes

victim
a person who suffers
because of a crime

X-ray
a type of radiation
that passes through
solid materials
that can be used to
examine bones or
organs inside a body

Index

Web Finder

www.all-about-forensic-science.com/science-for-kids.html
Test out your skills as a forensic pathologist with links to online
resources and games.

www.dogonews.com/2009/03/09/otzi-the-iceman-now-online
Learn more about the fascinating story of the Iceman.

http://library.thinkquest.org/04oct/00206/autopsy.htm
Discover the different clues that a dead body can reveal.

www.sciencenewsforkids.org/articles/20041215/Feature1.asp
Would you like to work as a forensic scientist? Find out more.